A CHRISTMAS TO REMEMBER
A Feast of Christmas Fun

A snowmobile raced across the snow and skidded to a halt outside a house in the North Pole. The radio mast was sending out a signal to say that someone was calling.

The rider jumped off the snowmobile and ran inside. He pulled off his furry hood and coat, and grabbed the headphones of the radio set to hear the voice at the other end.

"Hello? Hello?" came a familiar voice from the radio. "Is anyone there?"

The rider flicked a couple of switches on his radio set so that he could speak.

"Hello?" said the rider. "Can–you–hear–me?"

"**Yes, I can!**" chuckled Bob. "How are you, Tom. Are you still coming to stay with me for Christmas?"

"I'm fine … and yes, I'm coming for Christmas!" replied Tom.

"Fantastic! I can't wait," cried Bob. "See you soon, Tom."

"Wendy!" called Bob. "I've just spoken to my twin brother, Tom. And it's great news – he is definitely coming for Christmas."

"Oh, that's wonderful," said Wendy.

"This is going to be the best Christmas ever," cheered Bob, as he and Wendy did a twirl round the room.

"That reminds me, Wendy – have you seen my Santa Claus costume?"

"Not for about a year," joked Wendy.

Bob found the costume in the attic.

"It's a bit dusty," he said, as he went out into the yard. "I'll have to take it to the cleaners before I wear it on Christmas Eve."

"Er, hello Santa," giggled Lofty.

"Hey, everyone, I've got some great news," said Bob, excitedly. "My brother, Tom, who lives near the North Pole, is coming for Christmas!"

The machines all cheered.

"It's ages since I've seen Tom," said Bob.

"The North Pole is a long way away, isn't it?" asked Scoop.

"It certainly is," said Bob.

"Oh, I'd love to go there and meet Santa Claus," sighed Dizzy, dreamily.

"I'm sure you will, someday," laughed Bob. "But right now, we have a tree to put up in the town square."

"And we've got to get to the airport…" squealed Dizzy.

"…to meet Lennie and The Lazers!" added Roley. "Rock and roll!"

A delicious smell
was filling the
air at Farmer
Pickles's farm.

"Cor! Mince pies!
Yummy!" said Spud, who
was feeling very hungry.

"Morning, Spud!"
called Farmer Pickles.

"Mmm … mun … unyggg,"
replied Spud with a mouthful of pie.

"What are you eating?"
asked Farmer Pickles,
suspiciously.

Spud spun round to
hide the pies from Scruffty,
whose nose was twitching, but
Farmer Pickles saw them.

"Spud! Santa won't bring you
any presents if you're naughty!"
warned Farmer Pickles.

13

At the airport, Roley, Dizzy and crowds of photographers and reporters were waiting for the band.

"There they are!" called Dizzy.

"Hello, Lennie!" shouted Roley.

"How was the world tour?" asked a reporter.

"Cool … at-choo! Sorry – got a bit of a cold," said Lennie. "Yesss, very cool."

"What are your plans for Christmas, Lennie?" asked another reporter.

"We're doing a gig in the town square on Christmas Eve – don't miss it!" replied Lennie. "At-choo!"

"We won't!" cried Roley, rolling with excitement.

"Right, guys," said Lennie. "Let's get back to the studio and work on John's new song."

"Wow!" said Roley to John. "Do you write songs?"

"Yes," John replied. "But this last song is really tricky."

"Hey!" called Banger, the band's roadie. "Why don't you come and watch the band rehearse?"

"Rock and roll!" cheered Roley.

"Brilliant!" cried Dizzy.

In the forest on the edge of town, Bob and Wendy were choosing a tree to cut down. Spud had come along with Travis to help, and to be a really good scarecrow, after Farmer Pickles's warning.

"**Timbeeeerrr!**" called Bob, as a huge fir tree crashed to the ground. Lofty picked up the tree with his grabber.

"We'll take this to the town square, after we've planted these baby fir trees," said Bob.

"Why do we have to plant more trees?" asked Scoop.

"To make sure we'll have plenty of Christmas trees in years to come," said Wendy.

Over at the North Pole, Tom was packing for his trip.

"Right, Pogo," he said to his husky dog. "I'll need some socks, my best shirt..."

"**Woof,**" said Pogo, pointing his nose at Tom's toy elephant.

"What a clever husky!" praised Tom. "I mustn't forget to take Jumbo. Bob gave me this many Christmases ago, and when it broke, he fixed it with his very first tool set."

At Lennie's house, The Lazers were busy rehearsing for their concert.

"Sorry, guys – from the top again," said Lennie. But when he opened his mouth to sing, a big sneeze came out instead… "**Aaaaat-chooo!**"

"The gig's tomorrow night," worried Del, the bass player. "Lennie's got a bad cold and John, you haven't even started the new song." John went outside to find some fresh ideas.

"Hiya, John!" called Roley. "What's the matter?"

"I'm trying to write a new song, but it's really hard," sighed John. "I'd much rather be the singer in the band."

"Well," said Roley, "I find song ideas from the things I see around me."

John looked up at two squirrels in the branches of a nearby tree.

"Rockin' and a Rollin' squirrels, nah-nah, nah-nah!" he sang. "Hmm … I'm not so sure."

25

Bob brought the tree to the town square. As soon as he arrived, Mr Bentley pulled him into the town hall to meet the new mayor.

"Now, Bob," said the Mayor. "I'm trusting you with all of the town's Christmas celebrations – the lights need putting up, the stage needs building for the concert – and don't forget that you're Santa Claus again this year. Can you fix everything for us, Bob?"

Bob suddenly felt very hot. "Er, yes … er, I think so," he gulped. Tree, lights, concert – how could he get it all done?

Crash! Suddenly the Christmas tree smashed through the town hall window.

"Oh no! What's happened?" cried Bob, as he ran outside to see what was going on. Spud was hanging from the town hall clock, and the hands were bending with his weight.

"I was helping Lofty with the Christmas tree, but he lost control, and the tree went through the window, and I ended up here," moaned Spud. "Help!"

Bob looked up and sighed.

"Now I'm going to have to mend the clock, repair the window, put up the tree, the lights and build the stage…"

"**Can we fix it?**" asked Bob, wearily.

"**Yes, we can!**" shouted Scoop and Muck.

"Er, yeah … I think so," said Lofty.

29

Far away at the North Pole, Tom, Pogo and Scoot were racing to the harbour to catch the last boat. Suddenly, a baby reindeer ran across their path.

"Look out, Scoot!" called Tom. Scoot screeched to a stop.

"Have you lost your Dad?" Tom asked. The baby reindeer made a tiny crying sound.

Close by, there was a deep hole in the ice. Tom peered over the edge and saw the father reindeer, trapped on a ledge!

"We'll have to rescue him, Scoot," cried Tom.

"What about the boat?" said Scoot.

"We can't leave them – it'll be dark soon," replied Tom.

Tom put on his climbing gear and lowered himself into the hole. Slowly, with Scoot's help he hauled the reindeer up.

Once the reindeer were safely together, Tom and Scoot raced off. But when they came in sight of the harbour, they heard the boat's bell ringing.

"Oh, no, Scoot!" cried Tom. "We're too late! It looks like we won't be seeing Bob this Christmas after all," he sighed sadly, as they watched the boat sail off into the distance.

Back in the town square, Spud was skipping happily around a corner, when ... BANG! He bumped into Mrs Potts carrying sticks of rock, gingerbread and chocolate coins.

"Owww!" said Spud. "I'm really sorry."

"No harm done," said Mrs Potts. She started to pick everything up. "But you could help me with these decorations."

"Oh yes, yes, yessity, yes!" said Spud, remembering what Farmer Pickles had said about being a good scarecrow – he didn't want to miss out on any presents this year!

"Righto! You can get the fairy from the town hall cellar for me first, Spud," said Mrs Potts.

Mr Bentley led Spud into the cellar.

"I'll just take this box of decorations up for Mrs Potts," said Mr Bentley. "You look for the fairy, and don't touch anything else!"

As Spud was looking for the fairy, he spotted a top hat and tails, and just couldn't resist trying them on. He started to dance, and soon he found the perfect dancing partner, hiding behind a dust sheet – the Christmas fairy! But as Spud twirled around, he swung the fairy a little too fast, and suddenly her arm came flying off!

"Oh dear," moaned Spud. "What am I going to do?"

Bob and Wendy were back at the yard getting some tools. There was still lots to do, but everything was going smoothly.

"Miaoww!" said Pilchard, when she heard Bob's radio signal.

"That's strange," said Bob, "I wasn't expecting to hear from Tom again. You go ahead, Wendy. I'll catch up with you."

Wendy and the machines left to help set up the stage for the Lennie and The Lazers concert that night.

"Look – here comes Bob," said Wendy. "He'll help you fix the sound-check, Lennie."

Bob looked sad. Something was wrong.

"Tom's missed the boat," said Bob quietly. "He's … he's not coming for Christmas after all."

"Oh, Bob!" said Wendy.

"That's terrible!" said Lennie.

"Heavy!" said Banger.

"What's the story with Bob's brother, Wendy?" whispered Lennie.

"Well, he lives right up near the North Pole," Wendy explained. "So he'll never be able to get here for Christmas."

But Lennie had a cool idea.

"Come on, Wendy!" Lennie cried.

Dizzy had been listening to Wendy and Lennie.

"I wonder what they're planning," she said, with a cheeky glint in her eye.

"Well, Mr Bentley," said Mrs Potts, as they went down into the town hall cellar. "I think there's just one more decoration to put on the tree – the Christmas fairy."

"Here it is," said Mr Bentley. "Oof! It's much heavier than I remember! Now, where's Spud? I thought he was supposed to be our Christmas helper."

But they couldn't find Spud anywhere. Mr Bentley carried the fairy outside, and Lofty lifted it up onto the top of the Christmas tree.

"Lovely!" sighed Mrs Potts. "I love Christmas!"

"This is amazing!" said Wendy.

She was sitting next to Lennie in his private plane, and they were coming in to land near Tom's house in the North Pole.

"Woof! Woof!" barked Pogo far down below.

"Merry Christmas, Tom!" called Wendy.

"Wendy? How? Who? What?" said Tom, confused.

"Come on, Tom. We've got a Christmas party to get to!" laughed Wendy.

Tom ran inside to find his bag. As he was putting it in the hold of the plane, Dizzy popped out.

"What are you doing here?" Wendy asked, surprised.

"Well," said Dizzy. "I heard you and Lennie talking, and I thought I'd come along, too – to meet Santa!"

"It's Christmas Eve, and Santa will be busy getting his reindeer ready," Tom explained.

"We had better hurry," Lennie croaked. "I have to get back for the gig."

On the way back, Dizzy gazed out of the window.

"Oh, so lovely," she sighed. "The sun, the sky, the flying reindeer…" her voice trailed off, and she stared very hard into the distance. "Wow – it really is Santa!"

"Where?" asked Wendy.

"Over there!" said Dizzy, quickly. But Santa had flown by.

"Never mind," said Wendy. "You've reminded me about Bob's Santa costume. I must collect it from the cleaners. And it gives me a great idea…"

The sun was setting in the sky as Lennie's plane landed. Everything was ready for the concert. Lennie joined the band in the town square. He opened his mouth to say something, but nothing came out! He had lost his voice!

"Oh no," said John. "What are we going to do now?"

"Hey, John!" whispered Roley. "This could be your big chance."

"What do you mean?" said John.

"Well, if Lennie can't sing, you will have to," replied Roley.

"Groovy idea!" said Banger. "Rock on John!"

"Come on, everyone's waiting for the gig to start," said Roley. "Can you do it?" he asked.

"I … I don't know," said John, his knees wobbling.

Lennie went up on stage first and started the concert by playing his guitar. The crowd went wild!

"Rock and roll!" shouted Roley.

Then John stepped on stage and made his way to the piano. He looked amazing, dressed in a glittery suit and a pair of star-shaped shades.

The first song was the one that Roley had helped him write. It sounded great.

"**Yeaaaaaaaah!**" cheered the crowd.

"**Boogie on!**" called Spud from the top of the Christmas tree. He had been stuck up there, ever since Mr Bentley thought he was the Christmas tree fairy!

"Hey, let me down!" he shouted.

At the end of the concert, Bob suddenly remembered that he was supposed to be dressing up as Santa Claus and giving out presents to the children.

"Oh no…" he groaned.

"Ho, ho, ho!" said a familiar voice close by.

Bob stared. Who was this new Santa with a husky dog?

"Merry Christmas, everyone!" called Santa.

"And a special Merry Christmas to you, Bob," said Santa, as he handed Bob a blue toy elephant.

"**Jumbo?** How on earth? It can't be!" Bob exclaimed. "It isn't…"

"Oh, ho, ho, it certainly is," replied Tom.

"Tom! But how…? " Bob asked.

The two brothers gave each other a huge hug.

"It's fantastic to see you, Tom," said Bob. "But I haven't even done the shopping yet, and it's already Christmas Eve!"

"Nothing's changed, then," joked Tom. Wendy chuckled, "Don't worry, Bob. It's been taken care of."

"And now all we have to do is get Spud down," said Dizzy.

"Then we can all enjoy Christmas together," smiled Wendy.

Bob felt happier than he could ever remember.

"Thanks, Tom! Thanks, Wendy! Thanks, everyone!" he said.
"This really is going to be..."
"...the best Christmas ever!" laughed Tom and Bob together.

The End